RAPTORS!
HAWKS

Matthew Bates

PowerKiDS press.

New York

Published in 2016 by The Rosen Publishing Group, Inc.
29 East 21st Street, New York, NY 10010

First Edition

Editor: Sarah Machajewski
Book Design: Mickey Harmon

Photo Credits: Cover (series logo) Elena Paletskaya/Shutterstock.com; cover, pp. 1, 3–4, 6–8, 10, 12, 14, 16, 18, 20, 22–24 (border texture, fact box) Picsfive/Shutterstock.com; cover (background scene) M. Pellinni/Shutterstock.com; cover (falcon flying) aabeele/Shutterstock.com; cover (falcon perched) Bill Florence/Shutterstock.com; p. 5 Birdiegal/Shutterstock.com; p. 6 Robert Eastman/Shutterstock.com; p. 7 (vulture) Bunghiuz/Shutterstock.com; p. 7 (buzzard) Zdenek Kubik/Shutterstock.com; p. 7 (eagle) Praisaeng/Shutterstock.com; p. 7 (falcon) davemhuntphotography/Shutterstock.com; p. 7 (owl) Marcus R/Shutterstock.com; p. 9 Ondrej Prosicky/Shutterstock.com; p. 11 outdoorsman/Shutterstock.com; p. 13 LFRabenedo/Shutterstock.com; p. 15 (top) bmse/moment/Getty Images; p. 15 (bottom) Leonard Lee Rue III/Science Source/Getty Images; p. 16 © iStockphoto.com/roclwyr; p. 17 Todd Korol/Getty Images; p. 19 Robbie George/National Geographic/Getty Images; p. 21 Matt Gibson/Shutterstock.com; p. 22 Lindsey Eltinge/Shutterstock.com.

Cataloging-in-Publication Data

Bates, Matthew.
Hawks / by Matthew Bates.
p. cm. — (Raptors!)
Includes index.
ISBN 978-1-5081-4248-5 (pbk.)
ISBN 978-1-4994-1859-0 (6-pack)
ISBN 978-1-5081-4249-2 (library binding)
1. Hawks — Juvenile literature. I. Bates, Matt. II. Title.
QL696.F32 B38 2016
598.9'44—d23

Manufactured in the United States of America

CPSIA Compliance Information: Batch #BW16PK: For Further Information contact Rosen Publishing, New York, New York at 1-800-237-9932

Contents

The Mighty Hawk. 4

A Look at Raptors 6

Is It a Hawk?. 8

A Look at the Red-Tailed Hawk 10

Goshawks 12

Excellent Hunters 14

What's for Dinner?. 16

A Pair for Life 18

Humans and Hawks. 20

Special Birds 22

Glossary 23

Index. 24

Websites 24

The Mighty Hawk

Wild, open land is the perfect place to see nature in action. The plants, animals, and bugs in a **habitat** form their own world, where they depend on each other to survive. High in the air, one animal keeps watch over the activity below. It's the hawk.

Hawks belong to a group of birds called raptors. Raptors are skillful hunters, fast fliers, and often at the top of their food chain. Hawks are no exception.

> This hawk observes the world below from a **perch** high in the sky.

A Look at Raptors

There are about 10,000 species, or kinds, of birds in the world. Only a few belong to the raptor family. Raptors include hawks, falcons, eagles, owls, vultures, and buzzards. All these birds have features that make them raptors.

Raptors are carnivores, or meat eaters. They have sharp, hooked beaks they use to tear apart **prey**. Their feet have sharp claws, called talons. And they have excellent eyesight. All these features help raptors hunt.

hawk

Not every bird can belong to the raptor family. Just a small number of birds have the features that put them in this group.

RAPTOR FACTOR

Raptors are also known as birds of prey.

eagle

buzzard

owl

falcon

vulture

Is It a Hawk?

Hawks belong to a family of birds called Accipitridae (ak-suh-PIH-truh-dee). There are many species of birds in this family, including hawks, eagles, kites, harriers, and vultures.

True hawks are found on every continent except Antarctica. Hawks found in North America include red-tailed hawks, goshawks, sparrowhawks, and sharp-shinned hawks. These birds live in many kinds of habitats. They're most commonly seen flying over open land or nesting in trees. Some live in **marshes** or along mountain cliffs.

This goshawk uses its wings and feet to land safely on a tree trunk.

A Look at the Red-Tailed Hawk

The most common hawk in North America is the red-tailed hawk. How can you tell it apart from other raptors, and, more importantly, from other hawks?

The red-tailed hawk is larger than other hawks, which are usually known to be medium sized. Their **wingspan** ranges from about 45 to 52 inches (114 to 132.1 cm), and they weigh around 3 pounds (1.4 kg).

Red-tailed hawks are commonly brown, but they come in many colors. They often have a streaked **belly**. The top of their tail is the color of cinnamon, while the underside is pale.

RAPTOR FACTOR

Red-tailed hawks live throughout North America, from northern Canada down to Central America.

This red-tailed hawk has brown feathers, but some have blackish feathers, while others are pale or white. All red-tailed hawks have a tail that's a shade of red.

Goshawks

Northern goshawks are the largest true hawk in North America. They're known to be very powerful and **fierce**, especially when guarding their nest. They're mostly found in the northern forests of North America.

Northern goshawk wingspans are commonly between 40 and 46 inches (102 and 117 cm). They're light, weighing only up to 3 pounds (1.4 kg). These beautiful birds have brown feathers, but they can appear black or gray. Their belly and underside of their wings are pale and heavily spotted or striped. They have a white stripe of feathers above each eye.

The northern goshawk's beautiful coloring and fierce behavior set it apart from other hawks.

Excellent Hunters

Hawks are built to hunt. Red-tailed hawks have round, wide wings that are perfect for **soaring** on the wind. They're commonly seen circling in the sky, looking for prey. They also hunt from perches, keeping their eyes on the ground.

Northern goshawks hunt a bit differently. Their goal is to surprise their prey. They fly low to the ground, staying behind their prey so it doesn't see them. Nothern goshawks are known to chase their prey—both in the air and on foot.

RAPTOR FACTOR

A northern goshawk was once reported to chase a hare for almost an hour! They're also known to chase chickens until they can trap them.

red-tailed hawk

When hawks see a meal, they dive powerfully to catch it. Hawks keep their legs stretched out when they dive, which is different from other raptors.

goshawk

What's for Dinner?

Hawks have excellent eyesight, which makes them great hunters. Their eyes are made to help them judge distance, and they can see colors people can't. It's no wonder, then, that they're able to spot tiny prey from up in the sky.

What do hawks look for? They eat **mammals**, including mice, rats, rabbits, and squirrels. They also eat other birds, snakes, and **carrion**. Sometimes hawks hunt in pairs. When they catch their meal, they rip it apart with their sharp beak.

It's common to see hawks perched on telephone poles or fence posts near open fields and roads. They use this high location to find prey on the ground.

RAPTOR FACTOR

Hawks have to protect their kill from other raptors, which may swoop in to steal it!

A Pair for Life

Hawks keep the same partner for life. Both birds help build their nest. They build their nest in a high location, such as in a tree, alongside a cliff, or on top of a building. They build nests from plant matter such as tree bark and line them with softer matter such as leaves. Hawks use the same nest every year.

Nests are used for laying eggs. Female hawks lay between one and five eggs at a time. The eggs are white and spotted. Baby hawks hatch after around 45 days.

Baby hawks are born helpless and without feathers. Typically, male hawks hunt and bring food back to the nest, while the female sits on the nest and keeps her babies warm.

Humans and Hawks

     Hawks are naturally skilled hunters. A long time ago, people learned how to train hawks to hunt on command. This is the sport of falconry. Falconry was practiced in ancient China and medieval Europe, and is still popular today.

     Any kind of raptor can be used in falconry, but hawks are a popular choice for falconers in North America and Europe. Their **keen** eyesight and quick flying abilities make them great hunting birds.

> This hawk perches on its trainer's hand. Falconers have to wear thick gloves so their bird's sharp talons don't hurt them!

Special Birds

Hawks are special birds. Although they're much like other raptors, they stand out because of the way they hunt. They like to sneak up on their prey. They can dive and whip around **obstacles** to chase a fast-moving meal. They have no problem holding on to their place at the top of their food chain.

Hawks are very common in North America, especially near open fields. Next time you go for a drive, look up. Do you see a hawk?

Glossary

belly: Stomach.

carrion: A dead animal.

fierce: Likely to attack.

habitat: The natural home of a plant or animal.

keen: Very strong.

mammal: A warm-blooded animal that has a backbone and hair, and feeds milk to its young.

marsh: An area of low-lying land that is flooded and is usually wet throughout the whole year.

obstacle: Something that blocks a path.

perch: A place where a bird rests or sits. Also, to rest in a high location.

prey: An animal hunted by other animals for food. Also, to hunt an animal for food.

soar: To fly or rise high in the air.

wingspan: The measurement from the tip of one wing to the tip of the other.

Index

A
Accipitridae, 8

B
baby hawks, 18
beaks, 6, 16

C
carnivores, 6
claws, 6
colors, 10, 12, 16

E
eggs, 18
eyes, 6, 12, 14,
      16, 20

F
falconry, 20
feathers, 11, 12, 18
food chain, 4, 22

G
goshawks, 8, 12,
      14, 15

H
habitat, 4, 8

N
nest, 8, 12, 18
North America, 8,
      10, 12, 20, 22

P
perch, 4, 14, 17, 20
prey, 6, 14, 16,
      17, 22

R
red-tailed hawks, 8,
      10, 11, 14, 15

S
species, 6, 8

S
tail, 10, 11
talons, 6, 20

W
wings, 8, 12, 14
wingspan, 10, 12

Websites

Due to the changing nature of Internet links, PowerKids Press has developed an online list of websites related to the subject of this book. This site is updated regularly. Please use this link to access the list: www.powerkidslinks.com/rapt/hawk